BEYOND WINNING

Ultimate Guide in Navigating
Contentious Boardroom Meetings,
Resolving Corporate Conflicts and
Inspiring Others with Resolute Charisma

CHRIS LEO

INTRODUCTION

Welcome to a journey that will transform the way you navigate the dynamic world of corporate boardrooms. In the fast-paced realm of business, where decisions shape destinies and conflicts emerge, mastering the art of boardroom diplomacy is paramount. This ultimate guide is your compass, your ally in steering through contentious meetings, resolving conflicts, and leaving an indelible mark with unwavering charisma.

In the pages that follow, we unravel the mysteries of effective communication, strategic decision-making, and the subtle nuances that set great leaders apart. Whether you are a seasoned executive, an aspiring entrepreneur, or someone looking to enhance their leadership skills, this guide meets your need and solves your challenge.

The boardroom is not just a space for decision-making, but also a theater where leaders inspire confidence, increase collaboration, and ignite passion. We probe into the heart of corporate conflicts, offering practical insights and proven strategies to turn challenges into opportunities. Moreover, we explore the transformative power of charisma, providing you with tools to inspire those around you and leave a lasting impression.

As we embark on this journey together, remember that leadership is not just about titles; it is about influence and impact. The ultimate guide is your roadmap to becoming a dynamic, respected leader capable of steering any ship through the storms of corporate challenges. Get ready to elevate your leadership game and presentation skills. Making a lasting mark in the boardroom and beyond has never been that easy but this book provides the basics for achieving it.

Chris Leo

CHAPTER 1

UNDERSTANDING THE LANDSCAPE OF CONTROVERSIAL ISSUES

In the realm of debate, tackling controversial issues requires finesse and a deep understanding of the complexities involved. This chapter lays the groundwork for effective debate strategies by guiding you through the initial steps of topic selection, perspective exploration, and emotional intelligence.

Selecting a Controversial Topic

Choosing a debate topic is a strategic decision that sets the stage for engaging discussions. Consider your audience, their interests, and the societal relevance of potential issues. Aim for topics with multiple perspectives to ensure a dynamic and stimulating debate.

Factors to Consider

- Relevance to your audience
- Societal importance and impact
- Availability of diverse perspectives

Practical Action

- Brainstorm potential topics

- Research the current discourse surrounding each option
- Choose a topic that aligns with your audience's interests and has room for diverse opinions

Researching Perspectives

In-depth research is the cornerstone of a well-informed debater. To present a compelling case, it is essential to explore various viewpoints on the chosen issue. This section outlines effective research techniques and emphasizes the importance of relying on credible sources.

Research Techniques

- Utilize academic journals, reputable news sources, and scholarly databases
- Cross-reference information from multiple sources to ensure accuracy

Identifying Credible Sources

- Evaluate the author's credentials and expertise
- Check for peer-reviewed publications and well-established sources

Practical Action

- Create a comprehensive list of sources related to your chosen topic

- Systematically go through each source, extracting key perspectives and arguments
- Verify the credibility of each source to build a robust foundation for your debate

Understanding Emotional Triggers

Controversial issues often evoke strong emotions. Successful debaters are not only adept at presenting facts but also skilled in managing emotional responses. This section explores the emotional dimensions of contentious topics and provides strategies for addressing them during a debate.

Recognizing Emotional Hotspots

- Identify aspects of the issue that are emotionally charged
- Anticipate potential triggers for yourself and your audience

Addressing Emotional Responses

- Develop empathy to understand differing emotional reactions
- Tailor your communication style to foster a constructive emotional environment

Practical Action

- Create a list of potential emotional triggers related to your chosen topic

- Practice responses that acknowledge emotions while steering the debate towards rational discourse

This chapter serves as a foundational guide, equipping you with the tools to navigate the intricate landscape of controversial issues. As you proceed, remember that a well-informed and emotionally intelligent approach sets the stage for a compelling and persuasive debate.

CHAPTER 2

BUILDING A SOLID FOUNDATION WITH RESEARCH AND PREPARATION

Success in debate hinges on meticulous preparation. This chapter focuses on the critical steps of gathering compelling evidence, structuring persuasive arguments, and preemptively addressing potential counterarguments. By establishing a robust foundation, you enhance your ability to present a compelling and well-supported case.

Research Techniques

To construct a formidable argument, you must employ effective research techniques. This section delves into the intricacies of gathering information from reliable sources, fact checking, and ensuring the accuracy of your data.

Utilizing Online Databases and Academic Journals

- Explore reputable databases relevant to your topic
- Access scholarly journals to obtain well-researched perspectives

Fact-Checking and Verification

- Cross-reference information from multiple sources
- Verify data accuracy to fortify your arguments

Practical Action

- Compile a list of online databases and journals related to your topic
- Develop a systematic process for fact-checking and verification

Argument Construction

The strength of your debate lies in the coherence and clarity of your arguments. This section provides guidance on creating compelling and logically organized points to convey your stance effectively.

Crafting Clear and Concise Arguments

- Clearly articulate your main points
- Avoid unnecessary jargon or difficult language
- Organizing Points Logically:
- Structure your arguments in a logical sequence
- Ensure a smooth flow between different aspects of your case

Practical Action

- Outline the key points you want to convey in your debate

- Arrange these points in a logical order that enhances the persuasiveness of your argument

Anticipating Counterarguments

Anticipation is a key element of strategic debate. This section explores the importance of predicting counterarguments and provides strategies for developing robust rebuttals to address potential challenges.

Identifying Potential Challenges

- Analyze your stance from alternative perspectives
- Anticipate objections and counterarguments

Developing Strong Rebuttals

- Craft persuasive responses to potential challenges
- Present evidence and counterpoints effectively

Practical Action

- Role-play potential counter-arguments with a partner
- Refine your rebuttals based on feedback and further research

This chapter equips you with the tools necessary to construct a compelling and well-supported argument. As you delve into the art of debate, remember that a meticulously prepared foundation enhances your confidence and persuasiveness in the heat of discussion.

CHAPTER 3

MASTERING THE ART OF PERSUASION

Persuasion is the heart of a successful debate. In this chapter, we delve into the art of effective communication, the strategic use of rhetorical devices, and the cultivation of credibility to sway your audience. Mastering these elements is crucial for not only presenting a strong case but also leaving a lasting impact on your audience.

Effective Communication

The ability to communicate persuasively is a hallmark of a skilled debater. This section focuses on refining your public speaking skills, mastering tone and body language, and establishing a genuine connection with your audience.

Refining Public Speaking Skills

- Practice articulating your points clearly and confidently
- Pay attention to pace, tone, and modulation

Mastering Tone and Body Language

- Align your tone with the gravity of your arguments
- Utilize open and confident body language to enhance credibility

Connecting Emotionally with the Audience

- Use relatable anecdotes to establish a personal connection
- Appeal to the emotions of your audience without sacrificing rationality

Practical Action

- Record yourself practicing key segments of your debate

- Solicit feedback on your tone, body language, and emotional resonance

Rhetorical Devices

Rhetorical devices are powerful tools for constructing persuasive arguments. This section explores the strategic use of ethos, logos, and pathos, as well as employing anecdotes, analogies, and metaphors to enhance the impact of your message.

Incorporating Ethos, Logos, and Pathos

- Build credibility through ethos (ethical appeal)
- Present logical arguments through logos (logical appeal)

- Appeal to emotions through pathos (emotional appeal)

Using Anecdotes, Analogies, and Metaphors

- Incorporate personal anecdotes to humanize your arguments
- Employ analogies and metaphors to simplify complex concepts

Practical Action

- Identify key points in your debate where ethos, logos, or pathos can be strategically employed
- Experiment with incorporating anecdotes, analogies, and metaphors into your delivery

Credibility Building

Credibility is the foundation of persuasion. This section explores techniques for establishing yourself as a knowledgeable and trustworthy debater, including referencing authoritative figures and citing credible sources.

Establishing Expertise

- Showcase your knowledge on the topic through well-researched content
- Reference your own experiences or expertise related to the issue

Quoting Authoritative Figures

- Include quotes from reputable experts or authorities
- Attribute information to established sources to bolster credibility

Citing Credible Sources

- Emphasize information from well-established and respected sources
- Provide a clear and accurate citation of your references

Practical Action

- Compile a list of authoritative figures and credible sources relevant to your debate topic

- Integrate these references strategically into your arguments to enhance credibility

This chapter provides the essential tools for mastering the art of persuasion in debates. By refining your communication skills, leveraging rhetorical devices, and establishing credibility, you enhance your ability to influence and persuade your audience effectively.

CHAPTER 4

NAVIGATING CHALLENGING MOMENTS IN DEBATES

Debates are dynamic encounters that can present unexpected challenges. This chapter equips you with strategies for maintaining composure under pressure, tactfully addressing personal attacks, and adapting mid-debate to ensure that you stay on course toward a successful outcome.

Remaining Calm Under Pressure

One of the hallmarks of a skilled debater is the ability to remain composed, even in the face of challenging situations. This section explores practical strategies for managing stress and anxiety during debates, ensuring that you can think clearly and respond effectively.

Strategies for Stress Management

- Practice deep-breathing techniques to stay calm
- Develop a mental toolkit for handling stress in real-time

Maintaining Focus and Clarity

- Reframe stress as a normal part of the debating process
- Cultivate the ability to refocus quickly on the task at hand

Practical Action

- Develop a pre-debate routine to calm nerves
- Practice maintaining focus during simulated challenging scenarios

Addressing Personal Attacks

Debates can sometimes take a personal turn, with adversaries resorting to ad hominem attacks. This section guides you in responding tactfully to personal criticisms and redirecting the debate back to substantive issues.

Responding Tactfully to Ad Hominem Attacks

- Avoid responding in kind; instead, focus on the issues
- Acknowledge the attack without letting it derail the debate

Steering the Debate Back to Substance

- Direct the conversation back to the core arguments
- Emphasize the importance of addressing the issue at hand

Practical Action

- Role-play scenarios involving personal attacks with a debate partner
- Develop responses that redirect the conversation toward substantive issues

Adjusting Mid-Debate

Flexibility is a key asset in debates, where unexpected developments can occur. This section provides insights into recognizing when and how to adjust your approach, ensuring that you stay agile and effective throughout the debate.

Recognizing the Need for Adjustment

- Stay attuned to audience reactions and engagement levels
- Be responsive to shifting dynamics in the debate environment

Adapting to Unexpected Developments

- Modify your communication style based on audience feedback
- Adjust your arguments or strategy to address unforeseen challenges

Practical Action

- Practice debates with intentional disruptions to simulate unexpected scenarios
- Seek feedback on your adaptability from mentors or peers

This chapter prepares you for the fluid nature of debates, offering strategies to maintain composure, address personal attacks gracefully, and adjust your approach in response to unforeseen challenges. By mastering these skills, you position yourself as a resilient and effective debater.

CHAPTER 5

POST-DEBATE REFLECTION AND CONTINUOUS IMPROVEMENT

The journey of a debater does not conclude with the final words spoken in a debate. This chapter emphasizes the importance of post-debate reflection, seeking feedback, and committing to continuous improvement. By embracing a learning mindset, you pave the way for growth and excellence in your debating skills.

Reflecting on Performance

Reflection is a powerful tool for improvement. This section guides you through the process of analyzing your performance, identifying strengths, and pinpointing areas for refinement.

Analyzing Strengths and Weaknesses

- Assess your overall performance objectively
- Identify aspects of your debate that were particularly effective or lacking

Recognizing Successful Strategies

- Acknowledge tactics and approaches that worked well

- Consider how you can leverage these successes in future debates

Practical Action

- Keep a post-debate journal to document thoughts and observations
- Share reflections with mentors or peers for additional insights

Seeking Feedback

Constructive feedback is a valuable resource for improvement. This section outlines strategies for actively seeking feedback from mentors, peers, or judges and incorporating their insights into your skill development.

Gathering Constructive Criticism

- Request specific feedback on different aspects of your performance
- Encourage honest and detailed assessments from those with experience

Applying Feedback for Improvement

- Prioritize areas highlighted for improvement
- Develop an action plan to address feedback systematically

Practical Action

- Create a feedback form or questionnaire for post-debate evaluations
- Schedule regular feedback sessions with mentors or peers

Continuous Learning and Improvement

Debating is an evolving skill, and staying current is crucial. This section encourages a commitment to ongoing learning, staying informed on evolving perspectives, and dedicating time to refine your debating abilities.

Staying Informed on Evolving Perspectives

- Keep abreast of current events and changing societal views
- Update your knowledge base regularly to remain relevant

Committing to Ongoing Practice

- Schedule regular practice sessions to maintain and sharpen your skills
- Engage in mock debates on new and diverse topics

Practical Action

- Create a personalized study plan for staying informed on relevant issues
- Join debate clubs, participate in workshops, and engage in online forums to broaden your perspective

Congratulations on completing this comprehensive guide to winning debates on controversial issues. By embracing continuous improvement, you ensure that your debating skills not only thrive in the present but also evolve to meet the challenges of the future. May your journey as a debater be marked by growth, resilience, and the pursuit of excellence.

CONCLUSION

THE ORIGINALITY OF PERSUASION AND THE ENDLESS PROSPECT OF DEBATE MASTERY

In the tapestry of discourse, where ideas clash and opinions dance, your journey as a debater has been an exploration of intellectual prowess, emotional intelligence, and the artistry of persuasion. As we conclude this odyssey through the chapters of controversy, let us reflect on the profound insights gained and the path ahead illuminated by the flame of continuous improvement.

Anecdotes from the Arena

Consider the seasoned debater who, armed with facts and finesse, faced the tempest of disagreement with grace. It is in the crucible of contention that character is molded, and each well-articulated point becomes a brushstroke in the masterpiece of persuasive dialogue.

Recall the moments of triumph when a nuanced argument unfolded seamlessly, captivating the audience and leaving an indelible mark. Such anecdotes are the threads that weave the fabric of your debating legacy.

The Unseen Victory

In the realm of debate, victory isn't always tangible; it's not merely the points scored or the applause received. It's the subtle shift in perception, the seeds of doubt planted, and the minds swayed by the power of compelling rhetoric.

The true victory lies in fostering understanding, in sparking a collective curiosity that transcends the binary of right and wrong. An unspoken triumph echoes in the minds of the audience long after the debate has ended.

Embracing the Journey

Debating is not a destination but a journey, a perpetual quest for knowledge and refinement. Each debate is a chapter in the unfolding narrative of your growth—a story written with the ink of resilience, adaptability, and intellectual curiosity.

As you tread this path, remember that setbacks are stepping-stones, challenges are opportunities, and every argument, win or lose, contributes to the mosaic of your expertise.

The Never-ending Dialogue

In the grand theater of debate, the curtain never falls; the dialogue persists. The issues you grapple with today will evolve, and new controversies will emerge. Your commitment to continuous learning is your compass. Embrace the never-ending dialogue, and let the evolving discourse be your muse.

Parting Wisdom

In parting, remember that a debate won is not merely a battle of words but a triumph of understanding. Strive not only to persuade but also to be persuaded, for in the exchange of ideas, intellectual growth finds its fertile ground. Your words have the power to shape perspectives, influence opinions, and contribute to the collective wisdom of society.

I hope that your future debates be marked by eloquence, empathy, and the unwavering pursuit of truth. As you step off the debating stage, know that the journey continues—a journey of perpetual refinement and intellectual enlightenment.

In the immortal words of Socrates, "The only true wisdom is in knowing you know nothing." Embrace the humility of continuous learning, and let the symphony of your debates resonate in the corridors of intellectual history.

Go forth, noble debater, and let the echoes of your rhetoric reverberate through the annals of thoughtful discourse. The world awaits the eloquence of your ideas, the brilliance of your arguments, and the enduring impact of your intellectual legacy.